Gary's Lost

Today is Saturday. Mummy and Daddy are in their bedroom. Daddy is brushing his teeth. Mummy is sleeping. Gary goes into their bedroom.

Come on, Mummy. Time to get up. It's eight o'clock.

Gary! Stop! Your clock's too loud!

brushing

1

Gary opens the curtains. He looks outside.

Is it rainy outside?

No, it's dry.

Is it cloudy?

No, it's sunny.

Is it cold?

No, it's warm.

It's my birthday on Sunday.
Can I buy my birthday present today?

Yes!

Where's my watch?

curtains

2

Daddy is looking for his watch.

I can't find my watch. Can you see it, Gary?

Yes, Daddy. Look! It's under the table. It's on the floor.

What time is it?

It's ten to nine, Daddy.

Oh, my watch says a quarter past three.

The bus comes at nine o'clock. Come on. Let's go.

looking for

3

 **Puzzles**

1. Look at the pictures. Write the right words.

rainy   cloudy   sunny   cold

a)

It is _____.

b)

It is _____.

c)

It is _____.

d)

It is _____.

2. Where are the watches? Write the right words.

outside   under   on

a) Daddy's watch is _____ the box.

b) Mummy's watch is _____ the box.

c) Gary's watch is _____ the box.

Daddy, Mummy and Gary are at the bus-stop. Daddy is going to his office. Mummy and Gary are going to the toy shop.

Bye!

Bye!

Bye, Daddy!

Mummy, can I buy a clock, a robot and a game?

Gary, it's your birthday. You can buy one toy, but not three.

Inside the toy shop Gary looks at all the toys. There are dolls, robots, aeroplanes, bicycles, cars, rugby balls, footballs, basketballs, skateboards and games.

What time is it?

It's ten to ten now.

Can we buy this robot, Mummy?

Yes.

rugby balls

basketballs

Now Mummy, Gary and Rob are outside a cake shop. Gary is very happy. He likes his robot.

Mummy goes into the cake shop. She cannot hear Gary.

 **Puzzles**

1. What are they? Write the right words.

    a) You can ride a 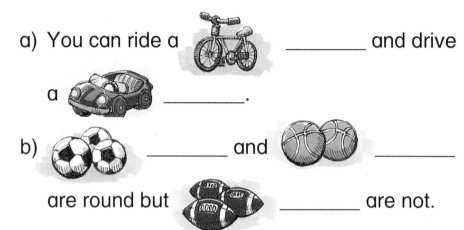 _____ and drive

    a _____ .

    b) _____ and _____

    are round but _____ are not.

2. Find these words in the word square.

robot

hundred

game

office

birthday

clock

A	W	K	L	J	M	G	E
B	I	R	T	H	D	A	Y
C	L	O	C	K	A	M	E
Q	R	B	O	A	T	E	S
U	X	O	F	F	I	C	E
H	O	T	O	D	A	Y	G
H	U	N	D	R	E	D	J
R	O	U	N	D	N	P	S

Gary is in the park. He is playing on a swing.
Mummy is outside the park. She cannot see Gary.

Gary was outside the cake shop. Now he is not there. Mummy looks in the toy shop. Gary is not there. Where is Gary? Can you see him?

Gary is in a tunnel.

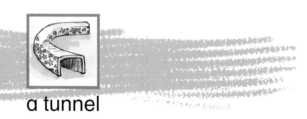

a tunnel

Gary and Rob like the park. They like the tunnels and the climbing frame.

What time is it, Rob?

It's a quarter to eleven.

Let's find Mummy.

Is my Mummy here?

Your Mummy was here, but now she's not.

tunnels

Puzzles

Read the sentences. Finish the clocks.

a)

It is seven o'clock.

b)

It is a quarter to eight.

c)

It is ten past one.

d)

It is half past five.

e) What time do you go to school?

I go to school at _____.

Gary and Rob go into the toy shop. Gary looks everywhere in the toy shop. He cannot see his Mummy. The shopkeeper sees Gary and Rob.

Where's your Mummy?

I can't find her.

Look! There's a policewoman. She can help you.

a policewoman

There are two policewomen. They help Gary.
They all look around the toy shop.

Is she your Mummy?

Her hair's the same but she's not my Mummy.

Is she your Mummy?

Her coat's the same but she's not my Mummy.

Can you see your Mummy?

No.

policewomen

Now the policewomen, Gary and Rob are in the street. They are looking for Gary's Mummy. Gary is sad. The policewoman talks on her radio.

Lost boy in Park Street. His name's Gary.

Yes, Gary's here. He's fine. Is his Mummy at the police station?

Yes, she is.

Good! We can come now.

Your Mummy's at the police station, Gary. Let's go.

 **Puzzles**

Look at the pictures. Write the right words.

coats   robots   five   three   radios   four

a) There are _____ boys, _____ women and
   _____ policewomen in the shop.

b) The boys have the same _____.

c) The women have the same _____.

d) The policewomen have the same _____.

The policewomen, Gary and Rob are outside the police station. Gary can see a woman inside.

Now Gary is inside the police station. He can see the woman's face.

Mummy is happy. Gary is happy, too. Mummy hugs Gary.

hugs

Mummy, Gary and Rob walk home. They are all very happy.

Mummy, thank you for my robot. I like it.

You're welcome.

His name's Rob!

That's a good name for a robot!

Hello, Daddy.

What have you got, Gary?

This is my new toy. It's a robot. You can call him Rob.

Puzzles

1. Look at the pictures. Write the right words.

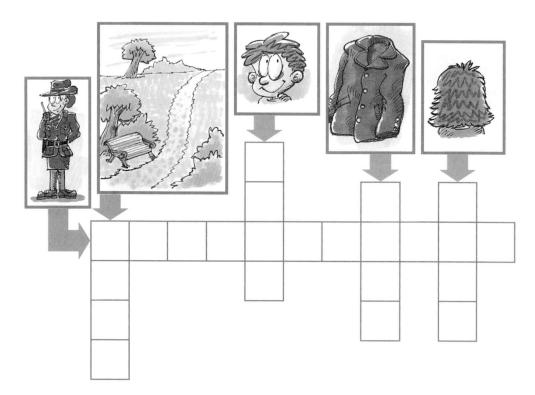

2. Read the sentences. Write the right words.

were   are   was

a) Gary _____ in the park.

b) Mummy and Gary _____ both lost.

c) Now Mummy and Gary _____ both in the police station.

Gary and Rob are in the sitting-room. Gary is playing with Rob.

What colour is my body?

It's green.

Yes, it is.

What colour are my eyes?

They're brown.

No, they aren't.

They're black.

Yes. You're right.

Mummy and Daddy come into the sitting-room.

Look, Mummy. Rob is a robot, a clock and a game. He can walk. He can talk. I can play with him.

Can I have a robot for my birthday, too?

Mummy, Daddy, Gary and Rob all laugh.

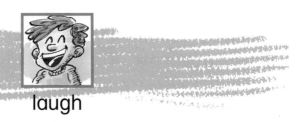

laugh

Questions

Page 1 a) What time is it?
       b) What is Daddy doing?
       c) What is Mummy doing?

Page 2 a) It is **dry/rainy**, **cloudy/sunny** and **warm/cold**.
       b) When is Gary's birthday?

Page 3 *True* or *false*?
       a) Gary cannot find his watch.
       b) Daddy's watch is under the table.
       c) Daddy's watch says ten to nine.

Page 5 a) Where is Daddy going?
       b) Where are Mummy and Gary going?
       c) How many toys can Gary buy?

Page 6 a) Where is Gary?
       b) It is ten **past/to** ten.
       c) Gary buys a _____.

Page 7 a) How much is the robot?
       b) What is the robot's name?
       c) Mummy goes into a _____.

Page 9 a) 'Let's go **in/to/on** the park,' says Gary.
       b) Gary is playing **to/under/on** a swing.

Page 10 a) Who looks for Gary?
       b) Where is Gary?

Page 11 a) What time is it?
       b) Is Gary's Mummy in the cake shop?

Page 13 *True* or *false*?
   a) Gary and his Mummy go into the toy shop.
   b) Gary cannot see his Mummy.
   c) Mummy is not in the toy shop.

Page 14 a) Who helps Gary?
   b) Can Gary see his Mummy?

Page 15 a) The policewoman talks **to/on/at** her radio.
   b) The policewomen, Gary and Rob are in _____ Street.

Page 17 a) Where is Gary?
   b) Who can Gary see inside the police station?

Page 18 a) Is Gary's Mummy inside the police station?
   b) Is Mummy angry?

Page 19 a) How do Mummy, Gary and Rob go home?
   b) Does Mummy like the robot's name?

Page 21 a) Where are Gary and Rob?
   b) What colour is Rob's body?
   c) What colour are Rob's eyes?

Page 22 a) Rob is a _____, a _____ and a _____.
   b) Who wants a robot for his birthday?